Jokes about Food

by Judy Winter

Raintree

www.raintreepublishers.co.uk
Visit our website to find out
more information about
Raintree books.

To order:

☎ Phone 0845 6044371
🖹 Fax +44 (0) 1865 312263
💬 Email myorders@raintreepublishers.co.uk

Customers from outside the UK please telephone +44 1865 312262

Raintree is an imprint of Capstone Global
Library Limited, a company incorporated
in England and Wales having its registered
office at 7 Pilgrim Street, London, EC4V 6LB –
Registered company number: 6695582

First published by © Capstone Press in 2011
First published in the United Kingdom in
paperback in 2012
The moral rights of the proprietor have been
asserted.

Consulting Editor: Gail Saunders-Smith
Editor: Catherine Veitch
Designer: Ted Williams
Studio specialist: Sarah Schuette
Studio scheduler: Marcy Morin
Production Specialist: Eric Manske
Originated by Capstone Global Library Ltd
Printed and bound in China by Leo Paper
Products Ltd

ISBN 978 1 406 24260 7 (paperback)
16 15 14 13 12
10 9 8 7 6 5 4 3 2 1

British Library Cataloguing in Publication Data
A full catalogue record for this book is available
from the British Library.

Acknowledgements
The author and the publishers are grateful
to the following for permission to reproduce
copyright material: all photos by Heinemann
Raintree (Karon Dubke), except: Shutterstock pp.
6 - background (ID1974), trucic background
design (throughout).

Every effort has been made to contact copyright
holders of material reproduced in this book.
Any omissions will be rectified in subsequent
printings if notice is given to the publisher.

Disclaimer
All the internet addresses (URLs) given in this
book were valid at the time of going to press.
However, due to the dynamic nature of the
internet, some addresses may have changed, or
sites may have changed or ceased to exist since
publication. While the author and publisher
regret any inconvenience this may cause
readers, no responsibility for any such changes
can be accepted by either the author or the
publisher.

Contents

Eggs, bacon, and fish, too

How did the egg get off the bus?

It used the eggs-it.

What do you get when you cross a pig and a centipede?

Bacon and legs.

Why did the hamburger join the running team?

Because it's fast food.

What happens to a hamburger that misses school?

It has to ketchup.

What do sea monsters
eat for dinner?

Fish and ships.

What did the sardine
call the submarine?

A tin of people.

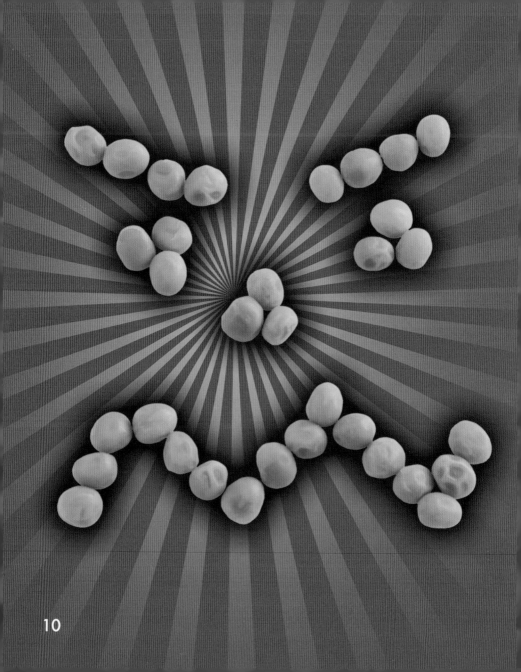

What do you call a
pea in a bad mood?

Grump-pea.

Why did the man put
veggies all over the world?

He wanted peas on Earth.

What is the difference between broccoli and a bogey?

Kids won't eat broccoli.

What is the strongest vegetable?

A muscles sprout.

What do you call two banana peels?

A pair of slippers.

Why did the banana go to the doctor?

It wasn't peeling well.

Why do potatoes make good detectives?

Because they keep their eyes peeled.

What country was the first to fry potatoes?

Greece.

What's a firefighter's favourite soup?

Min-nee-nar-stroni.

What kind of soup never gets hot?

Chilli.

What food talks
a lot?

A talk-o.

What kind of food is
always cold?

A burrr-ito.

What is a frog's favourite drink?

Croak-a-cola.

How do you make a milk shake?

Scare it.

Further reading

Horrid Henry's Mighty Joke Book,
Francesca Simon (Orion Children's Books, 2008)

Sidesplitters: Champion Crack-ups,
(Macmillan Children's Books, 2012)

Create your own joke

Follow these steps to write your own joke:

1. Pick a topic. A one-word noun is good.
   For example, "cow".

2. Make a list of words connected to your topic
   - "udder", "pat", "calf", "bull", "moo", and words
   that rhyme with those words and your topic -
   "shudder", "half", "full".

3. Make a list of joke types. For example:
   "Why did the ... cross the road?"
   "What did the ... say to the ...?"

4. Try out different jokes, fitting your words from step
   2 into the joke types from step 3. For example,
   "Why did the cow cross the road?" "To get to the
   udder side!"